FEB   2006

EXTREME SPORTS No Limits!

Extreme Motocross

Bobbie Kalman & John Crossingham

Crabtree Publishing Company

www.crabtreebooks.com

Created by Bobbie Kalman

Dedicated by Katherine Kantor
To Adam and Alex, the best boys in the world

Editor-in-Chief
Bobbie Kalman

Writing team
Bobbie Kalman
John Crossingham

Substantive editor
Niki Walker

Project editor
Kelley MacAulay

Editors
Molly Aloian
Amanda Bishop
Rebecca Sjonger
Kathryn Smithyman

Art director
Robert MacGregor

Design
Katherine Kantor

Production coordinator
Heather Fitzpatrick

Photo research
Crystal Foxton

Consultant
Kerry Graeber, Vice President and Director of Communications,
AMA Pro Racing

Photographs
Photos provided by American Honda Motor Corporation:
    back cover, pages 5, 10-11, 17, 18, 30
AP/Wide World Photos: pages 6, 7, 8
Steve Bruhn: pages 13 (top), 15, 16, 19, 21, 22, 29
© Tony Donaldson/Iconsportsmedia.com: page 23
Mark Kariya: pages 13 (bottom), 24, 25, 26, 27
Paul Martinez/PHOTOSPORT.COM: page 28
Shazamm: pages 9, 20
Photo courtesy of Yamaha: page 31
Other images by Corbis Images

Illustrations
Bonna Rouse: page 12

Disclaimer: Neither the publisher nor the author shall be liable for any bodily harm that may be caused
or sustained as a result of conducting any of the activities described in this book.

Crabtree Publishing Company

www.crabtreebooks.com   1-800-387-7650

PMB 16A
350 Fifth Avenue
Suite 3308
New York, NY
10118

612 Welland Avenue
St. Catharines
Ontario
Canada
L2M 5V6

73 Lime Walk
Headington
Oxford
OX3 7AD
United Kingdom

Cataloging-in-Publication Data
Kalman, Bobbie.
    Extreme motocross / Bobbie Kalman & John Crossingham.
        v. cm. -- (Extreme sports no limits series)
Includes index.
Contents: What is motocross?--Early motocross history--Motocross
today--Anatomy of a bike--Safety first--Motocross courses--Course
racing--Supercross--Motocross freestyle--Freestyle competitions--
Enduros--Trials riding--Stars and legends--Motocross for beginners.
    ISBN 0-7787-1670-8 (RLB) -- ISBN 0-7787-1716-X (pbk.)
    1. Motocross--Juvenile literature. 2. Extreme sports--Juvenile
literature. [1. Motocross. 2. Motorcycle racing. 3. Extreme sports.]
I. Crossingham, John. II. Title. III. Series.
    GV1060.12.K35 2004
    796.7'56--dc22
                                                              2003024983
                                                              LC

CONTENTS

Enduro races are held on unpaved tracks.

Motocross or "MX" is a daring sport that features skilled motorcycle riding. Motocross is mainly an **individual sport**, which means that riders perform alone. Team motocross events are also popular—they allow riders to perform as members of a team. Some MX competitions are races, whereas others feature tricks that test riders' skills.

MOTOCROSS STYLES

The name "motocross" refers to motorcycle races held outdoors on dirt, grass, or sand **courses**, but there are other styles of motocross, as well. **Supercross** competitions are held indoors on tracks constructed in large stadiums. **Freestyle** motocross is not about racing at all. This style involves giant ramps and jumps that launch riders high into the air, where they perform tricks. Many motocross racers also participate in other motorcycle events, such as **enduros** and **trials riding** or "trials." Enduros are long-distance outdoor races that test a rider's **endurance**. Trials riding tests a rider's ability to ride slowly over **obstacles**, or objects, without falling.

No Free Rides

No matter which style riders choose, they need great balance, strength, and skill to master their sport. Many of the best motocross riders are **professionals** or "pros," which means motocross is their job. They constantly challenge themselves to race faster and perform riskier tricks. Pros are so daring that they have helped make motocross an **extreme sport**. Extreme sports test the limits of their athletes.

Even with proper training and safety equipment, motocross can be a risky sport. Riders race around tracks at great speeds or fly high into the air with their bikes.

EXTREME DANGER

The athletes shown in this book perform many daring stunts and tricks, but they had to train for years to master their sport. Only professionals should attempt these risky moves and riding styles.

EVERYBODY SCRAMBLE!

In the late 1800s, the motorcycle was a new invention. It changed the way many people traveled on roadways. Riders soon discovered that they could take their motorcycles off the roads, too. The earliest off-road motorcycle events were held in Britain between 1910 and 1930. Racers tested their skills by riding up and down steep hills and over natural obstacles.

LET'S RACE!

By 1924, British riders were holding off-road motorcycle races, called **scrambles**, all over the countryside. For an even greater challenge, some racers pushed themselves to finish long, demanding scrambles—and enduros were born. Riders in France and Belgium soon began holding scrambles, too. They called the new sport "motocross." This name was a combination of the French word "motocyclette" and the English term "cross-country."

Although the name "motocross" was coined in the 1930s, riders in Britain, the United States, and Canada called the sport "scrambles" until the 1960s.

A DIFFERENT WAY OF RACING

In the 1930s, off-road races spread across Europe. They were held on courses that had been designed instead of on rough country trails. In 1947, the **Fédération Internationale de Motocyclisme** (**FIM**) established the first motocross championship.

SPREADING THE WORD

By the 1950s, motocross was an organized sport throughout Europe. At that time, most American races were casual scrambles or enduros held for fun by local motorcycle clubs. In the 1960s, however, European motocross stars began traveling to America. The European riders had incredible turning and jumping skills that amazed American motorcyclists. American riders became more interested in motocross and began entering world competitions. In the early 1970s, the **American Motorcyclist Association** (**AMA**) held the first modern motocross races in the United States.

In the 1970s, motocross racing gained popularity in the United States.

NEW TIMES, NEW STYLES

Early motocross races were held in rural areas. People had to make long drives and plan whole weekends just to attend a race. Spectators crowded along the edges of the course to catch a glimpse of the riders, since there was no seating. In 1972, motocross got a boost in popularity when someone thought of bringing the races to the spectators. Competitions were then held at stadiums and **speedways** in or near large cities. People loved the comfort of watching motocross from stadium seats. Thanks to these competitions, supercross was born.

FIERCE RIVALRY, LONG DISTANCES

Throughout the 1970s, both North America and Europe began hosting enduros that covered 1,000 miles (1609 km) or more! The intense competition between riders from these two continents made motorcycle sports more popular throughout the world. Before long, American motocross racers were competing against the top riders from European countries, and the skills of American riders quickly improved. By the 1980s, the United States was home to many of the best motocross riders in the world.

FREE FALLING

Extreme sports became very popular in the 1990s. Many of these sports centered around ramps that launched athletes into the air, where they performed tricks. Inspired by what they saw, MX riders soon tried their own versions of these high-flying moves. They called the new sport freestyle motocross. Freestyle quickly received support from highly promoted events such as the **X Games** and the **Gravity Games**. Freestyle has helped bring MX many new fans, and the sport is now more popular than ever.

Spectators love watching motocross athletes perform daring freestyle tricks.

TIMELINE

1867: American Sylvester Roper builds the first steam-engine motorcycle

1885: the first gas-powered motorcycle is invented by German Gottlieb Daimler

1904: the FIM is founded

1910: early trials take place in Scotland and England

1924: the first scrambles are held in Britain

1924: the American Motorcyclist Association is founded

1947: the FIM holds the world's first official motocross race—Motocross des Nations—in France; teams of MX racers compete for the title

1957: the FIM holds a motocross world championship for individual riders

early 1960s: European racers travel to America to promote motocross

late 1960s: more female racers begin competing in the U.S.

1971: the AMA holds a motocross event at Daytona Speedway in Florida

1972: the AMA begins holding stadium supercross events across America

1975: the first Women's National Motocross championships are held

mid 1980s: motocross racers are seen performing tricks during practices; these tricks help lead to freestyle MX

early 1990s: motocross racers begin performing tricks during their races

1996: the **Women's Motocross League** (WML) is formed to help promote women's racing around the world

ANATOMY OF A BIKE

Motocross motorcycles are also called **MX cycles**, **dirt bikes**, and **trail bikes**. They are lightweight and built to take a beating. The bikes have **engines** of various sizes to suit different riders and motocross styles.

Engine sizes are measured in **cubic centimeters** or "cc." The larger the engines are, the more power they have. For example, 500cc engines are much more powerful than are 125cc and 250cc engines.

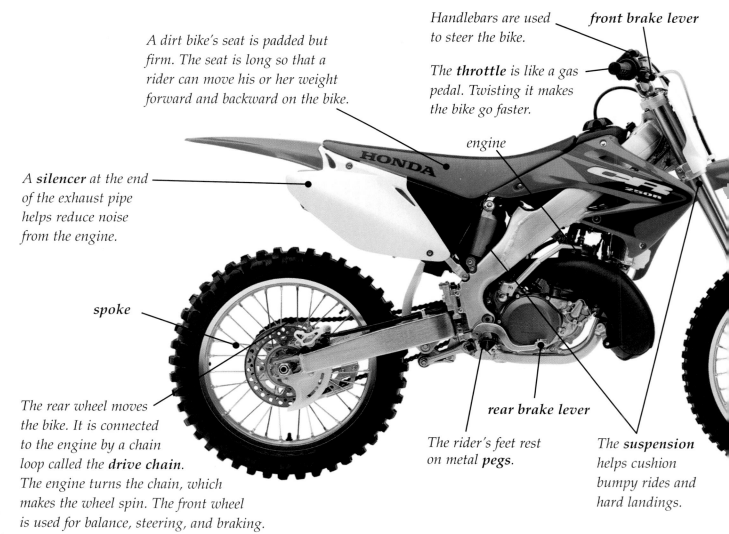

A dirt bike's seat is padded but firm. The seat is long so that a rider can move his or her weight forward and backward on the bike.

Handlebars are used to steer the bike.

front brake lever

*The **throttle** is like a gas pedal. Twisting it makes the bike go faster.*

engine

*A **silencer** at the end of the exhaust pipe helps reduce noise from the engine.*

spoke

*The rear wheel moves the bike. It is connected to the engine by a chain loop called the **drive chain**. The engine turns the chain, which makes the wheel spin. The front wheel is used for balance, steering, and braking.*

rear brake lever

*The rider's feet rest on metal **pegs**.*

*The **suspension** helps cushion bumpy rides and hard landings.*

Bigger isn't Better

Until the 1960s, European companies such as CZ and Husqvarna were the main manufacturers of dirt bikes. Their motorcycles had powerful engines, but the bikes were large, heavy, and difficult to control around tight corners and over large bumps. In the late 1960s, Japanese companies, including Suzuki, Yamaha, and Honda, began making dirt bikes.

These bikes were much smaller and lighter than the European bikes. Their light weight made turning easier, which meant riders had more control than ever while riding. As a result, courses started becoming more difficult, and **aggressive riding** such as freestyle eventually became possible. Today, Japanese bikes are the standard in motocross, but some European brands are still popular.

Fenders block flying mud and dirt kicked up by the spinning tires.

*Wheels are made of steel. Rubber tires fit on the wheels and are filled with air. The tires have a bumpy, grooved surface called a **tread**. An MX tread is designed to grip dirt and prevent slipping on racetracks.*

Hit the Brakes!

There are two **brakes**—one on the front wheel and the other on the rear wheel. The front wheel brake is controlled by a lever near the right handlebar. The back wheel brake is controlled by a lever in front of the right foot peg.

Gearing Up

Most dirt bikes have five **gears**. The gears on a dirt bike are similar to the gears on a bicycle—there are low gears and high gears. Different gears affect the speed of the bike by changing how fast the rear wheel spins. The higher the gear, the faster the rear wheel spins. Low gears turn the wheel slowly but with a lot of force. A bike always starts out in first gear, and then the rider can **shift up** to higher gears. To change gears, the rider first has to pull in the **clutch**. The rider then changes gears with the **gear lever**.

SAFETY FIRST

Motocross can be a dangerous sport, and even the best pros sometimes fall. All riders need excellent safety equipment to protect themselves from injuries. This equipment can be hot, heavy, and awkward, but no one rides without the required gear shown here. Young riders also need adult supervision to keep them safe.

*If a helmet doesn't have a visor, the rider wears **goggles** to keep dirt out of his or her eyes.*

body armor

TOUGH CLOTHES

An MX **jersey** and pants help protect the skin, if a rider is thrown from the bike. These clothes are made of flexible, durable materials such as leather and **synthetic**, or artificial, fibers. They must be tough enough to withstand sliding along rough and rocky ground without tearing or shredding.

HARD HEAD

The **helmet** is the most important piece of MX safety equipment. It is a hard plastic shell with a soft padded liner. A **visor**, or eye shield, blocks the sun. A face protector guards the rider's jaw. Helmets must fit snugly—a loose helmet could shift and block the rider's view.

Gloves protect the hands and help give the rider a better grip on the handlebars.

BODY ARMOR

Tough plastic body armor protects a rider's chest, shoulders, shins, knees, elbows, and forearms. The armor should be snug but not too tight.

Most MX boots are made of leather and plastic. They are padded and have a metal toe for extra protection.

STAYING ALERT

Respect is the key to safety in motocross. Riders must respect one another, whether they are practicing, racing, or just riding off-road for fun. They must always be aware of other riders and bystanders. Riders must also look out for rocks, holes, tree stumps, and other hazardous obstacles. A collision with any of these things can leave both riders and bystanders injured.

DAILY CHECKUP

Dirt bikes may be light, but they are powerful machines that can cause serious injuries. Riders must continuously maintain their bikes to keep them in safe working order. Before every race or practice run, a smart rider inspects his or her bike for problems. Motorcycles have many parts, and a problem with even one of them can cause an accident. Most daily inspections involve a quick check of the brakes, spokes, drive chain, and fuel levels. The **tire pressure** is also checked, as it greatly affects the bike's **stability**, or balance. Serious riders have their entire bikes checked every few weeks.

Collisions with other bikes can be dangerous. Riders must always be aware of their surroundings.

During long races such as enduros, a team of mechanics helps maintain the bikes.

13

FOLLOW THE COURSE

A motocross course has many twists and turns. The racing surface is usually dirt, mud, or grass. Most courses range from half a mile (0.8 km) to two miles (3.2 km) long. Regular motocross courses feature natural hills, bumps, and turns, so each course is different and has its own challenges.

Some courses have artificial bumps and obstacles, as well. To begin the race, riders line up at the **starting line**. The starting line is wide enough to fit up to 40 racers side by side. The course narrows soon after the start, and it becomes more difficult for racers to pass one another.

DIFFERENT SURFACES

Dirt is the usual surface for motocross, but racers have to be able to ride on grass, mud, and sand, as well. Grass allows riders to go quickly, but it's very slippery. It also wears away—a course could be grass at the start of the day and mostly dirt by the end! When it rains, a dirt course becomes sticky with mud, slowing down the riders. Sand is the trickiest riding surface. It is soft and difficult for tires to grip. Racers can easily get stuck going uphill. If they do, they have to get off and push their bikes.

RACE FOR THE FINISH

Depending on the race, a rider may have to ride around a course for 20 or 30 **laps**! A lap is one trip around a course.

Races can have any number of laps, depending on the track. On the final lap, the winner is the first racer to cross the **finish line**. A checkered flag is waved to declare the winner.

*The track narrows at the **first turn** on every MX course.*

starting line

finish line

*Most tracks also include a **whoop** section.*

*A raised part of the course is called a **jump**.*

*A turn with a **banked**, or raised, edge is called a **berm**.*

15

THEY'RE OFF!

Winning a motocross race requires more than speed. Racers **strategize**, or plan moves, to pass other racers. Riders need to make quick starts and have good balance, smooth turning skills, and calm nerves. Even a small mistake can cause a rider to lose the lead and fall behind.

*First gear uses so much power during the start of a race, that the bike can **pop a wheelie**, or rise up on its back wheel. Riders lean forward on the bikes to prevent wheelies.*

THE HOLESHOT

If a racer has the **holeshot**, it means he or she is the first racer to reach the first turn in the course. The racer with the holeshot often wins the **moto**, or race. To get the holeshot, a racer must use the clutch, gear shift, and throttle properly to get the bike up to top speed quickly. **Dead-engine starts** make getting a holeshot more challenging. During these starts, racers cannot start their engines until the race begins.

GET IT IN GEAR

Riders shift gears to suit each stage of the moto. All tracks require different gearing. Riders often begin in first gear to get strong pushes. They quickly shift into second, then third, then fourth, and finally fifth gear. Riders may spend much of the race in fifth because it is the fastest gear. If they need more speed to get up a hill, they will downshift into second or third gear to gain power from the engine.

TURN IT UP

Getting around turns fast and with control is also important in winning races. The **inside line** is the shortest distance around a turn. Most racers like to be near the inside line, even though this position requires a lot of braking. Racers usually avoid the **outside line**, especially when they are behind other racers. Not only is the outside line the longest path around a turn, but racers on it can be pushed easily off the course.

AND THE WINNER IS...

Most motocross competitions do not decide a winner from just one race. Instead, the competition is broken down into two motos. Each rider races in both motos and receives a score based on how he or she places. Low scores are the best, so the rider who places first gets the lowest score. The overall winner is the racer who has the lowest total after the scores from each moto have been added together.

Sharp turns require a lot of braking, whereas wide turns need little or no braking. Instead of braking, the racer leans into a wide turn.

SUPER DUPER

Stadium floodlights allow supercross events to be held at night. Motocross races generally take place only in daylight.

Supercross races are just like motocross races, but the courses are built in stadiums and have no natural obstacles. Dirt is hauled into a stadium by dump trucks and then shaped into a course by bulldozers and other heavy machines. Supercross courses often have more jumps than motocross courses have.

WHOOP, WHOOP!

Since supercross obstacles are all made by people, they can be larger and more creative than motocross obstacles. Common supercross obstacles are whoops or "whoop-de-doos." They are usually in groups, constructed close together to test a biker's balance and jumping abilities. With enough speed, bikers can jump over more than one whoop at a time.

CAUGHT IN A RUT

Every course eventually gets **ruts**, but they are especially common in supercross. Ruts are thin, deep grooves that form when many racers ride over the same spots. Ruts usually form near the inside line of a turn or on a steep bump, where tires dig in hard. They get deeper with every tire that rides over them. Eventually, wheels can get stuck. Racers sometimes have to avoid a spot on the course that they would like to use because it has large ruts.

A good way to avoid the ruts that have formed near the inside line is to ride on the outside of a berm. Racers lean into the turn to maintain their speed and balance.

FEELING FREE

The newest style of motocross—freestyle—may be the most exciting of all. Freestyle riders do not race against one another. Instead, these athletes fly high into the air with their motorcycles to perform tricks.

GETTING AIR

Riders use giant dirt ramps and curved wooden ramps to help them get as much **air**, or height, as possible. It is common for riders to be over 30 feet (9 m) in the air! Once airborne, riders pose, spin around, and hang off their bikes in various positions. Freestyle tricks are known as **aerials** because they take place in midair. The positions of both the body and the bike are important in an aerial. After the trick is performed, the rider must be ready to land quickly.

There are hundreds of different aerial tricks, and new ones are being invented all the time.

FINE ADJUSTMENTS

MX bikes are often adjusted for freestyle tricks. The seat cushion is lowered so riders can easily swing their legs back and forth over the bike. Panel cutouts and grab handles are added to the rear and the front of the bike. These adjustments allow the rider to get a firm grip on different parts of the bike during a trick. The pegs are often made longer to improve the rider's footing. Once these changes are made, all the rider needs is a ramp and a lot of guts. Above is an example of just how spectacular aerials can be.

FREESTYLE FACE-OFF

Most freestyle competitions have three categories—freestyle, **big-air**, and **step-up**. Freestyle riders get up to 90 seconds to perform creative aerials on a course full of different ramps. They have to complete as many tricks as possible before their time runs out. Big-air and step-up riders want to get as much air as they can.

AMAZING THE JUDGES

The series of tricks performed by a rider is called a **routine**. The tricks in a rider's routine must be challenging in order to impress the judges. Some riders have a balanced routine, with several equally difficult tricks, whereas others perform a few extremely tough aerials to amaze the judges.

THE BIG TIME

The big-air event is similar to freestyle, but riders can perform only one aerial. They are given two chances to launch themselves from a giant ramp. The ramp is designed to give the riders the most **hang time**. Hang time is the amount of time a bike spends in the air. Since there is only one trick, riders usually save their most impressive aerial for the big-air competition.

TAKE IT UP

A step-up competition doesn't involve fancy tricks. To win, bikers just need to get air—a lot of it! A step-up features a tall, steep ramp. At the top of the ramp is a bar. The rules are like those for a track-and-field high-jump competition, but in step-up, the bar can be more than 30 feet (9 m) high! The bar usually starts at around 22 feet (6.7 m). Each rider who clears the bar gets to move to the next round, when the bar is raised by one foot (0.3 m). These rounds continue until the riders can no longer clear the bar.

ENDUROS

Enduros are very challenging races. Motocross racers often participate in them to train for future MX races. Enduros are so long, that bikers must tackle all sorts of conditions and surfaces before reaching the finish line. Enduros take place on a variety of landscapes—including forests, deserts, and mountains. Some are day-long races, but the longest, called **rallies**, can last three weeks! Longer enduros are broken down into day-long sections called **stages**. These enduros often have classes for cars and trucks, as well as motorcycles. Racers must be able to **navigate**, or find their way through, the course because the trails are unmarked.

READY FOR ANYTHING

Enduro courses are also unpredictable, which makes it difficult for racers to strategize. Surprises wait around every bend. Stages in forested areas are especially dangerous. Racers must leap over rocks, weave among trees, and fly down steep hills as quickly as possible.

In order to win an enduro, the rider must watch the bike's fuel level carefully.

THE LONG HAUL

More than speed is needed to win an enduro. An enduro is about staying strong over a long period of time. Riders wear so much equipment, that they sweat a lot, which can **dehydrate** and weaken them. To prevent dehydration, the riders carry water pouches with drinking tubes so they can drink while riding. Enduro riders must also know how to fix any problems that arise with their bikes during races, such as flat tires or snapped drive chains.

WELL TRAVELED

Two of the most famous enduros are also among the longest—the **Dakar** and the **Baja 1000**. The Dakar traditionally runs 5,282 miles (8500 km) from Paris, France, to Dakar, Senegal. To complete the route, competitors and their bikes must be shipped across the Mediterranean Sea! As the name suggests, the Baja 1000 runs 1,000 miles (1609 km) along the Baja Peninsula in Mexico. This area is very hot and dry. The conditions can cause riders to become **fatigued**, or extremely tired. Many riders are forced to quit as a result.

The Baja 1000 is North America's longest and most famous enduro.

GOING ON TRIAL

Trials riding is another way for motocross racers to keep in shape for future events. It is the slowest motorcycle competition there is. The object is to ride across large **ravines**, or narrow valleys, and over obstacles such as logs without stopping or putting a foot down.

TAKE IT SLOW

Trials courses are so tricky, that riders move their bikes slowly. The slower a bike moves, however, the more likely it is to tip over. Trials riders need incredible balance and control to avoid falling. Engines also tend to **stall**, or stop, if they are driven too slowly. To prevent stalling, trials bikes have **crawler gears** that are lower than a standard dirt bike's first gear.

It may not be flashy, but trials riding is a great test of skill.

WHAT'S THE JUDGMENT?

Trials courses are split into different sections, based on their difficulty. Some sections are so difficult, that they are less than 100 feet (30 m) long. Easier sections are about a half-mile (0.8 km) long. During a competition, judges award riders points for completing certain sections of the course. Trials riders can also lose points for incorrect form. If the bike stops moving forward, the rider loses five points. If the rider places a foot down to balance the bike, he or she loses one point.

*Placing a foot down to balance the bike is called **dabbing**. Dabbing is against the rules.*

Trials events may not attract as many spectators as supercross, but people can get much closer to the action.

27

STARS AND LEGENDS

Motorcycle racing has a rich history of almost one hundred years. In that time, many riders have come and gone, but a few have become legends. The riders on these pages are famous for shaping their sport and for performing tricks never before done on dirt bikes. They have all attracted fans to the many styles of motorcycle racing and competition.

ROGER DECOSTER

Belgian great Roger DeCoster (above right) is the father of modern motocross. DeCoster started his career as a world trials champion before becoming more involved in motocross racing. In the 1960s, he helped bring motocross from Europe to the United States. In the 1970s, he was an unstoppable racer who won 37 **Grand Prix** events—a world record that still stands. He went on to become a manager of Team USA and Team Honda, leading them to many victories. DeCoster currently manages Team Suzuki. In 1994, DeCoster was inducted into the Motorsports Hall of Fame of America.

JOHN DESOTO JR.

Nicknamed "The Flyin' Hawaiian," John DeSoto Jr. was a major force in motocross for over 30 years. He began riding in the late 1960s, winning several U.S. motocross championships. At a time when European riders such as Roger DeCoster dominated the sport, DeSoto won world MX titles in 1971 and 1972. He went on to become a great enduro racer, winning competitions well into the mid 1990s. He entered the Motocross Hall of Fame in 1997.

RICKY CARMICHAEL

Florida native Ricky Carmichael (shown right) is the king of motocross. He's only 5'4" (163 cm), but his record packs a serious punch. He has several national championships and, in 2002, he became the only MX racer in the history of the AMA to go undefeated for an entire season. His name appears in motocross magazines, movies, and even in video games. Many fans call him the Michael Jordan of motocross.

JAMES "BUBBA" STEWART

James "Bubba" Stewart has always been faster than anyone on a motorcycle! After winning nine AMA Amateur titles, Stewart became a pro in 2002. He quickly won his first supercross title and was named Rookie of the Year. Bubba is the first African-American to dominate his sport. His outstanding abilities inspire young people everywhere to start up a bike and tear up the course.

STEFFI LAIER

German racer Steffi Laier could be one of the best female motocross riders ever! After winning many German championships in the late 1990s, she was the WML champion in 2001, 2002, and 2003. Laier began racing at the age of six and was only eighteen when she won her latest championship! It seems her days at the top have just begun.

Motocross is an exciting sport that kids as young as six can start to learn. There are many motocross clubs that can help future racers get a proper start. If you want to follow in the footsteps of the pros, make sure you use common sense. Motocross can be a dangerous sport, so you always need supervision! A good instructor will keep a watchful eye on you and help prevent an injury.

Look in your phone book or do a web search for local instructors and clubs. A motocross summer camp is a great place to learn more about the sport. It allows you to spend part of your summer holiday training with skilled instructors.

A motocross school or camp, such as the one shown above, features all types of courses to improve your MX riding skills.

PINT-SIZED BIKES

If you are younger than ten, a standard dirt bike will probably be too large for you. Instead, you can buy a **mini-bike**. Mini-bikes have smaller frames than regular bikes have, and their 50cc engines are less powerful. They make it safer and easier for you to learn how to control a motorcycle. There are even mini-bike MX leagues found in some parts of the United States.

FOR MORE INFORMATION

The curious motocross fan has a lot of places to discover more about the sport and its stars. Magazines such as *Dirt Bike* and *Transworld Motocross* offer great information on motocross tricks, techniques, and events. Your local library may also have books on the sport. The internet is full of great sites dedicated to motocross. You'll find a starter web list below. Have fun!

MX SITES!
www.transworldmotocross.com/mx - a great online MX magazine that also features other extreme sports
www.expn.go.com/mtx - the home of the X Games includes bios, event reports, and a full glossary
amaproracing.com - the AMA's official motorcycle racing site

Mini-bikes such as this 50cc Yamaha let young riders get used to off-road riding.

GLOSSARY

Note: Boldfaced words that are defined in the text may not appear in the glossary.

aggressive riding A style of riding based on daring tricks

brake A device on each motorcycle wheel that, when pressed, reduces the bike's speed

clutch A device for smoothly connecting and disconnecting the driving parts of a motorcycle

course A mapped-out trail for racing

cubic centimeter A unit of measurement that equals the size of a one-centimeter cube

dehydrate To lose great amounts of water, resulting in weakness and exhaustion

endurance The ability to handle stress and difficult circumstances

engine A machine that powers a motorcycle

gear A part that enables an engine to move

gear lever A moving part that changes the gears of a motorcycle

Grand Prix An annual series of motocross races in which each race takes place in a different country

Gravity Games An annual series of extreme sports competitions

jersey A tight-fitting shirt made of heavy materials worn by a motocross rider

speedway A course used for car or motorcycle racing

tire pressure The force of air exerted on the tire tube; more air results in firmer tires, less air results in softer tires

X Games A series of extreme sports competitions held twice a year

INDEX

1 2 3 4 5 6 7 8 9 0 Printed in the U.S.A. 3 2 1 0 9 8 7 6 5 4